T0171128

The Revelation OF Lucifer

His Fall from Grace to Disgrace

Thomas Jones

WestBow
PRESS
A DIVISION OF THOMAS NELSON

Copyright © 2013 Thomas Jones.

All rights reserved. No part of this book may be used or reproduced by any means, graphic, electronic, or mechanical, including photocopying, recording, taping or by any information storage retrieval system without the written permission of the publisher except in the case of brief quotations embodied in critical articles and reviews.

WestBow Press books may be ordered through booksellers or by contacting:

WestBow Press
A Division of Thomas Nelson
1663 Liberty Drive
Bloomington, IN 47403
www.westbowpress.com
1-(866) 928-1240

Because of the dynamic nature of the Internet, any web addresses or links contained in this book may have changed since publication and may no longer be valid. The views expressed in this work are solely those of the author and do not necessarily reflect the views of the publisher, and the publisher hereby disclaims any responsibility for them.

Any people depicted in stock imagery provided by Thinkstock are models, and such images are being used for illustrative purposes only.

Certain stock imagery © Thinkstock.

ISBN: 978-1-4497-9965-6 (sc)
ISBN: 978-1-4497-9964-9 (e)

Library of Congress Control Number: 2013911505

Printed in the United States of America.

WestBow Press rev. date: 6/28/2013

Acknowledgments

I would like to take a moment to praise God and thank Him for allowing me to receive this revelation, for without His desire to give us more insight into this very important area, we would still be in the dark.

How can anyone say that God doesn't fully love him or her? I want to thank His Son Jesus Christ for His willingness to put on sinful flesh, come down to earth, and become the sacrifice that would satisfy what the Father required when man fell.

Also, I'd like to thank the person of the precious Holy Spirit for being everything Jesus said He would be in our lives.

I would now like to take a moment to personally thank Gloria Jones, my wife, that sweet, darling woman of God whose unwavering prayers and intercessions throughout our twenty-five saved years of marriage, through the help of the Holy Spirit, have richly blessed my life in a way that words can't explain. Her willingness to suffer and prevail in everything Satan has brought our way is beyond description. I personally saw and know all the times Satan has tried to destroy her and sift her like wheat, but through it all, she's always determined to prevail. Please don't mistake my taking this moment to recognize her as lifting her up, because I'm not. The Bible says to give honor to whom honor is due. I'm just taking the time on one of those rare occasions to show her my godly appreciation of her for all the things she's done and for what she has meant to me personally. Since 1983, she has always been totally surrendered to the Lord. I'm sure there are countless women who also fit this description, though I've never personally known them, nor anyone whose life was so Christlike. She's always been willing to do whatever it takes to have victory in the kingdom, no matter the cost. We've been attacked in every area and arena of life, yet she's never fussed. There were times when we didn't know what we would eat or how we would make it, but somehow she was always able to take nothing and make something for the family to eat. The Devil has attacked her for just about the entire twenty-five years she's been saved, targeting her health, finances, children, ministry, and family, yet by God's grace she has prevailed. There has always been a strong demonic attack on our lives almost from the start. Even when I didn't see or know, she was right there prevailing in God. I've seen her at her weakest moments when it seemed like Satan would win, but she always fought and went on. Even when she didn't know how, by the grace of God she made it through. God has placed her by my side in this lifetime for so many reasons, all of which all are blessings. She's been my teacher, intercessor, prayer partner, fasting buddy—everything that I needed in each of those moments of my life. One day God will allow me to really show her how so very much I appreciate and respect her. So I just thought it important to take the time to recognize the woman who has stood by my side from the very start. Again, the Word says to give honor to whom honor is due, so Gloria, my Pet-Pet, I'll love you always and forever.

I want to thank my niece Veronica for taking this book in its sloppy state and transforming it into what you're reading today. Veronica, you're such a sweet, unassuming, soft, sincere woman of God, and I love and appreciate you very much.

I also want to thank Veronica's mother, Minnie, who, when she first received our call via her sister Gloria asking her if Veronica wouldn't mind editing and placing in proper manuscript form

The Revelation of Lucifer, immediately said, "Sure." Next to her sister Gloria, I think she is one of the sweetest, gentlest, sincerest, and most loving Christians I've ever met, and I say to you, Minnie: Thank you so very much.

Thomas Jones

Foreword

The revelation of Lucifer was given to me in the spring of 2007. It's very hard to explain what happened to me, but I will do my best to share it with you.

I was talking with someone one day about the different Christian movies that were out and their varying portrayals of things in the Word of God. We also discussed how no movie really ever discussed Lucifer and how he upset and changed the human race. *The Ten Commandments* showed Moses, and *The Greatest Story Ever Told* and *Jesus of Nazareth* both portrayed Jesus. *The Passion of the Christ*, I think, offered another perspective, as we were to see all of the sufferings of Christ. As we spoke, my friend and I touched on several parts concerning the little-known figure who was the major player in the fall of man.

Then something strange happened to me the moment our conversation ended. It was like all rest was taken from me, and more thoughts kept entering my mind concerning Lucifer. For the next two days I was very uneasy in my spirit, and I couldn't understand why. Soon after, I realized that God was allowing me to see in my spirit everything concerning Lucifer's rise and fall. I can't explain it, but it was like He put everything concerning Lucifer into my spirit and mind all at once.

Until now, I was a little apprehensive, because this was all different and new to me. When I realized He was giving me a revelation about Lucifer, at the same time I knew He wanted me to share it with believers and nonbelievers alike.

Now as for me, I love to write, and way back in the 1980s I

wanted to write a book concerning my spiritual life. I did start it, but soon it just faded away. Those of you who write would agree with me on this. When you're writing, a certain spirit comes over you, giving you the urge to write as long as that spirit lasts, but when it leaves, the desire to continue to write passes away. Well, that spirit to write was with me from time to time in the 1980s, but then it would leave again. It has been over a decade since the spirit to write has come upon me to write. Then, when God began to show me this revelation, something happened, because even before I picked up the pen, a strong urge came over me to write. This time it was different, because as soon as I picked up the pen, I couldn't keep up with the information He was placing in my spirit. It was like He had shown me everything at once concerning Lucifer, and all I had to do was write it down.

This may sound strange, but it was revealed to me as I wrote. It was so amazing to me. It was as if I had already experienced everything He was giving me to write. This blew my mind, because though it was as if I'd already seen it, it was revealed to me as I wrote.

I don't know why He chose to reveal it to me in the way that He did or why He even gave me this revelation of Lucifer in the first place. I do believe now that He wanted this information to be shared with everyone everywhere. Why me? For what purpose? I can only say that I believe He wanted to reveal Lucifer to us in a way that's never been seen before.

I know some of you will be saying, "Yeah, but why Lucifer? Of all the persons in the Holy Bible, why him? Why not God, Jesus Christ, the Holy Spirit, or even one of the heroes of the Bible? Why not Michael or Gabriel?" I can only admit that I don't know. I'm sorry I can't answer those questions. All I know is what He put in my spirit and my mind to write, and that is exactly what I'm doing—writing *The Revelation of Lucifer*. There's nothing

I could say that would put to rest the skeptics or critics and their perception of this. I'm doing what I know the Holy Spirit has revealed to me in my spirit. All I ask of you is to pray earnestly and sincerely before and while reading this book. I'm convinced that if your heart is right and your motives are pure, you will receive a witness in your spirit concerning this book.

I want to give glory, honor, and praise to my God and Father, to His precious Son, Jesus Christ, and the person of the Holy Spirit. Seeing this revelation and having the ability to put it on paper are true blessings, and I will praise and magnify Him forever. My desire and purpose are and have always been to do His will, no matter what, and to be found faithful concerning the tasks He has assigned me.

I still sometimes ask myself why He loves us so much and cares for us so. What did we ever do to deserve what He has done for us? He loved us so much that He sent His only begotten Son to die in our place for our sins. We should be ever so grateful for the love of the Father and equally as grateful for Jesus Christ, who willingly chose to put on sinful flesh, come down to a sinful world, and become our sacrifice by being crucified in our place, bringing us back into right fellowship with the Father. I also thank the Holy Spirit for coming just like Jesus said He would and empowering us to live like Christ, which brings glory to the Father.

Chapter 1

In order for readers to fully comprehend what's about to happen, I must share this in the way it was revealed to me. From the moment it was given to me, it was as if I had seen everything in my spirit. I can't explain it except to say that I was inspired to tell you this very important part of God: Lucifer and his great fall. I personally think that, for the most part, the church as a whole has refused to delve into or at least take a closer look at this. I think our lack of information on this subject and willingness to dig deeper has been a detriment to our knowledge of Him. We'll quickly show you what we believe to be the areas of the Bible that speak to and reveal everything about the Trinity, which is so very vital, as we must give all the glory to the godhead. But for some reason, we're ignorant of the downfall of the entire race.

It is perfectly all right if you do not believe me when I say that the Holy Spirit inspired me to go into an area of the Bible never before touched in the way that He gave it to me. I do believe that, at the completion of this book, you will come to understand Him better than you do now. Things that maybe aren't as clear before you read the book will now be much clearer.

The area that I was inspired to write about is simply Lucifer, Satan, the Devil.

After the Lord saved my wife and me in 1983, for the next twenty years we were raised and brought up in an apostolic, Pentecostal church where Lucifer's names were never mentioned, other than when reading the Bible or rebuking him for one thing or another. It was a cardinal sin to ever mention his name in any other context. The Word of God says people perish for a lack of knowledge. If Lucifer weren't so important, he would never have been mentioned as much as he is in the Word. After all, it was he who caused us to be in the mess that the world is in today. He is the root cause. If there were no Devil, we would still be experiencing the joy of life in the garden of Eden, living in the dispensation of innocence. But the truth is that's not the case.

If we're to learn from what happened to this once great archangel, cherub, and worshipper of the godhead, we have to be willing to put our preconceptions to the side so that we can be open and honest enough for the Holy Spirit to bring us to a position to gain much-needed insight. Plus, we could learn from his mistakes and thus strive for a life that's more pleasing in the Father's sight. It is also important that we understand why Lucifer had such deep hatred and disdain for God.

Hopefully, this book will cause those who don't know him to make a decision that will determine their destiny.

Secondly, I pray that the believer will be inspired to commit to the kingdom of God and all His righteousness. Thirdly, I pray that those Christians who have fallen away or slid backward will repent, do their first works over, and get back into their assigned destiny.

I give all the glory to God the Father, for allowing the Holy Spirit to touch me in a way that I'd never ever experienced before.

Can you imagine seeing something in its entirety, step-by-step, as if you had actually been there? I already know that some will believe and some won't. That's not my concern. My assignment is to give it to you just as He gave it to me. I'd simply ask the Holy Spirit to lead and guide you through every page of this book and to quicken your spirit as He has quickened mine. I humbly ask for your prayers for my family and me so that we will always yield to the will of the Father so that we will be pleasing to Him in all that we do.

I do believe one of the reasons the Holy Spirit revealed these things to me is that we are so close to the end that you can almost taste it. The Lord will soon come back, and the church needs to be ready for that one last great revival that will usher us to be with Him forever. I believe the only purpose of this last revival is to bring men and women into their proper places, both nonbelievers and believers. And when that has happened, He will appear like a thief in the night and receive His bride. So sit back and enjoy what the Holy Spirit has very strongly put on my spirit.

Chapter 2

How can you explain the beauty of heaven in words that would adequately describe the majesty and glory that are seen there? If you were exposed to something incomparable to anything on the earth, you'd just stand in awe of the majestic splendor of the workmanship of God's power. I simply can't explain, other than to say Michelangelo, in all his gifts of the arts, doesn't even come close to describing the artistic beauty and splendor of heaven. You can only comprehend that the same God who created the great beauty of earth—all the elements—designed the place where He would abide with His angelic host. Heaven is full of all types of activity. There's always movement and something taking place. Angels are everywhere, and their beauty is beyond description. I know we get a glimpse of angels in Revelation, but there are truly trillions upon trillions of them. Their magnificence, their strength, their splendor—what a sight to behold. The archangels, cherubim, and seraphim, common angels, and living creatures all have a purpose, and each does different things according to the will and purpose of God.

There seems to be so much oneness. No one is displaying anything that doesn't glorify God the Father. There's no sense of who's greater, who has the most ability, who can move, or even who's closer to God. No. None of these things ever existed, and that's incredible. It's just perfect oneness and togetherness, and everyone seems to be so humble. It's the type of humility no one has ever seen. It's difficult to explain, but in all that they do, there seems to be a type of worship and praise that's always toward the Father. Everything that's going on seems to bring glory to God. What's so amazing is that with such a large host of angels around, everyone appears to have his or her own responsibilities, and whatever they are, they simply glorify God.

I noticed that different angels are always going back and forth between the different levels of heaven. The vast majority of conversations are about the splendor of God. They constantly lift and praise Him and give Him glory without tire.

There is an absolute peace and security beyond description. Heaven itself glorifies God in everything. Every part of heaven somehow points back to the awesome splendor and power of God. Everyone and everything gives glory to God. It's as if you can know without seeing that all of heaven exists simply to glorify God.

Although the same thing seems to happen over and over again, each day seems to be different, and you never get tired or bored with what you're watching. No two days are ever the same, and each new day is greater than the last. You apparently reach a level where you feel as if you can't take more of the beautiful, marvelous display of workmanship and worship and are just about to burst with joy, exuberance, ecstasy, and everything else that's wonderful. You are thinking, *This is it,* yet the next day takes you to an even higher level.

I think that if this took place on earth while we were still in our physical bodies, it would be too much, and we would all faint, unable to stand it. What we do here on earth, in terms of worshipping, praising, and giving glory to God, just does not compare to what's going on in heaven. Could you imagine if in church all we did was worship, magnify, and praise God? In the beginning, it would be fine. But probably after the second week, people would get tired and want to do other things. Thank God that He's giving us the time to practice here on earth so that when we finally do get to heaven, it will be automatic. The book of Psalms says to let everything that has breath praise the Lord.

I also noticed that, in spite of the innumerable angels in heaven, I could still distinguish each individual angel. Soon after that, I noticed two angels had a certain awe about them. They seemed different from the rest, with a different stature and authority. All of the other angels, without really being noticeable, apparently had a great admiration for these two. They were awesome to look at, a very powerful, beautiful sight to behold, yet they were so very, very humble. By their demeanor, you wouldn't think that they were anything more. They were always assisting the other angels. There was a presence about them that caused the entire heavenly atmosphere to worship and praise God more. Everything about them suggested the glory of God, and their entire existence brought glory to God. Whenever they showed up, it seemed to automatically ignite a higher reverence for God. There was something about them that displayed a brightness that the other angels (though they had a glow) didn't have. And given their absolute humility, only because you could see that brightness would you know that they were on a different level.

I also noticed that there were different places in heaven where the angels would go to be before the Father. I don't know how, but every angel, although in God's presence, couldn't go but so far into the different levels. Even so, each level seemed to feature something different about His presence. Though every angel stopped at different levels, there was no difference in God, yet there was a difference.

Now here on earth, if this took place, there would be splits, divisions, and lots of jealousy over who was allowed to go where. Some would be bragging, while others would be envious of their brethren. That's why in heaven, although it's there, somehow it doesn't matter, for the worshippers' behavior and character do not change.

I soon came to realize that those two angels were Michael and Gabriel and that they had a special place in God.

I became aware that the angels were always talking about a certain angel, always making references. They would have questions that they wanted answered, and they always agreed to wait until he showed up. Though they wanted to do certain things or ask the Father certain questions, they would always decide to wait until "he" showed up, for he will know what to do, how to do it, or even how to present it to the Father.

At times heaven itself would erupt with the sound of music, and the angels' expressions would show that they knew or had seen something that had brought on this ecstatic rejoicing. I would always wonder what this was and what it meant.

Then, one day, as I enjoyed the beauty and splendor of heaven, I heard that excitement and watched the effect it had on heaven, but this time it was getting louder and louder. And as I turned around, I saw Michael and Gabriel, who looked so superior to everyone else. Then, to my surprise, Michael and Gabriel started joining in with the other angels. They were worshipping someone, but for someone. And then he appeared. He looked simply awesome—like nothing I'd ever seen before.

Chapter 3

I think now it's important to examine angels and their positions in heaven.

The word *angel* comes from the Greek word *angelos*, which means *messenger*. One dictionary defines an angel as "a member or order of heavenly beings who are superior to man in intelligence and power."

Information on angels can be found three hundred times in Scripture. As a matter of fact, they are mentioned in every book of the Bible except Ruth, Nehemiah, Esther, John's epistles, and James.

We know that there are five divisions of angels. In the Bible, you can find 104 appearances of angels, who are sent to help and direct the lives of men.

Angels are constantly at work in heaven. Most of their time is spent praising and worshipping God.

In Joshua 5:13–15 an angel appeared on earth, and again in Genesis 18:14, I Kings 19:5–6, Psalm 78:25, Mark 16:5, John 20:12, 1 Corinthians 4:9, 1 Corinthians 13:1, Isaiah 6:1–30, Matthew 18:10, Revelation 5:11–12, Revelation 7:11–12, and Luke 20:36. All of these references show the appearances of angels and their actions.

Now let's examine the five different ranks or divisions of

angels, beginning with archangels. *Arch* means "chief," which tells us that there are different ranks. This word *archangel* is used only twice in the Bible, both times in the New Testament: 1 Thessalonians 4:16 and Jude 9. We already know of two archangels: Michael and Gabriel. *Michael* means "he who is like God." Michael always appears in times of war or battle. He is seen in Daniel 10:13, Daniel 10:21, and Revelation 12:7–8.

The name *Gabriel* means "mighty." He is God's messenger. This angel we can find in Daniel 8:16–17, Daniel 9:21, Luke 1:19, and Luke 26:27.

Many people don't know that Lucifer also was an archangel. Lucifer's name means "holder of light." Isaiah 14:12 says concerning him:

> Thou hast been in the garden of God (this was the first Eden). Every precious stone was thy covering and thy pipes was prepared in thee in the day that thou was created. Thou art the anointed cherub that covereth and I have set thee so. Thou was upon the mountain of God. Thou has walked up and down in the midst of the stones of fire. Thou was perfect in thy ways from the day that thou was created.

Ezekiel 28:13–15,18 shows he was also a priest: "Thou has defiled thy sanctuaries." This amazing archangel held two offices: archangel and cherub. There's only one other being in heaven who holds more than one office, and that is Christ.

The position of the godhead is as follows: God the Father, God the Son, and God the Holy Spirit. And then there's Lucifer. Lucifer was honored above all other angels. He was privileged to walk back and forth before God. The stones of fire are where

God's glory resides. (Remember, when Israel saw God, they saw stones of fire.) He was perfect in beauty and wisdom. As a matter of fact, he was perfection itself. He was the worshipper of the godhead. Whenever he spoke, an orchestrated sound would come from him. I'll stop there for now, but I'll revisit Lucifer in a little while.

There are four other divisions of angels aside from the archangel. They are the common angels, the cherubim, the seraphim, and the living creatures. Common angels minister to God's people. They hear God's voice and carry out His commands. See Hebrews 1:14. Seraphim are angels who stand over God's throne in heaven and declare His holiness. An example is found in Isaiah 6. The seraphim do not have the power to take away iniquity or to purge sin, just the power to pronounce the forgiveness of sin and iniquity on the Lord's behalf. Cherubim were represented by the two golden figures of two-winged living creatures. They are all of one place with the golden lid of the ark of the covenant in the Holy of Holies, signifying that the prospect of the redeemed and glorified creatures was bound up with the sacrifice of Christ. They represent redeemed human beings in union with Christ, proceeding out of the mercy seat, suggesting a consciousness of the union Christ has produced. They are first seen in Genesis 3:24. This protection of the tree represents the Lord's protection of our salvation. Refer to Ezekiel 1:10. Living creatures are similar to the cherubim, but they have one head with eyes all around. They have six wings. One living creature was like a lion. One had a calf's face, another had a man's face, and one was like an eagle in flight. They minister in heaven by worshipping and glorifying God. See Revelation 4:6–9 and Revelation 19:4-15:7.

Chapter 4

Now let's get back to Lucifer. Not only was he made unlike any other angel, but he had a very strong and commanding presence. Even Michael and Gabriel seemed to be affected by his presence and beauty, in a very good way. Lucifer's presence somehow glorified God the Father—it alone seemed to do something to heaven itself. The following is a very poor example, but it is the best one I can come up with. It's like a pinball machine in that when the ball is hit, every instrument in the machine—all the lights and sounds—comes alive. He was something you can't accurately describe in words. You could spend countless thousands of years just looking at his beauty. In a way it was as if his appearance was constantly changing, over and over again. There were colors you've never seen before. Whenever he moved, things would just react, akin to putting French fries into a pot of boiling oil—as soon as the fries hit the oil, there's an atomic reaction in the pot. As beautiful and exquisite as the other angels were, especially Michael and Gabriel, Lucifer stood out. There was one strange thing: in spite of all his beauty, he was so very, very humble. He was also one of the few angels who were allowed to walk up and down before God on the throne. And each time he came out, he would be more radiant and spectacular than before. He seemed to love to spend most of his time in God's presence.

The next spectacular thing about him was that whenever he opened his mouth, there would be music that came forth like nothing you could even fathom hearing. This music sounded like a trillion-man orchestra—an orchestra whose music you could listen to forever. Whenever he brought forth his music, it seemed to do something to everything in heaven—angels, elements, the whole makeup of heaven. It was so powerful and commanding. What was really incredible was that whenever he played, even God on His throne seemed pleased. It was as if you could feel that God was smiling in complete satisfaction. Still, in spite of all this, Lucifer seemed and acted extremely humble and unassuming. He was always trying to help out wherever and whenever he could—always worshipping, praising, and giving God the glory. Everything he ever did always pointed back to God. I'd never seen this type of humility displayed before. It seemed as though everyone was always coming to him with questions for him or for God. They would wait for Lucifer to come, and then they would get his advice or get him to take a message to God.

Although Lucifer would play music whenever he was walking in the presence of God, he would also play in the various parts of heaven, but he was happiest whenever he was before the throne. Being before the throne just seemed to excite him in an awesome way. I soon realized when I didn't see him, it was because he was on earth with one-third of the angels in Eden. Don't panic. I'll show you in Scripture that this is all true. This Eden was as beautiful as the second garden of Eden where Adam and Eve lived. This is called the pre-Adamic Eden. Every type of prehistoric animal that we see in our history books existed here. The only difference is that they were not wild, nor were they brutes. They were all like sheep. They were very tame, and there was no threat to any kind to any animal, large or small. There seemed to be a gentle peace and serenity among these animals. Every animal appeared to be able to cohabitate in perfect harmony. There were nations and kingdoms of angels everywhere. In this garden of Eden, Lucifer's responsibility was to give the worship of the earth to God and to give the laws of God to the earth. I saw a beautiful sanctuary in the midst of the garden where Lucifer would go to carry out these duties. He would spend so much time in the sanctuary of God, praising, worshipping, and giving Him glory, and I soon understood that somehow he was able to take all the worship and praise of the angels into the sanctuary and offer them up to God. All of the angels stood by whenever he went in and waited. Whenever he did this, beautiful music played, and you just knew that God accepted it. He would come out of the sanctuary, and without saying a word, he would somehow relate the laws of God to angels in a way that they understood, and then they would all start worshipping and praising God in approval. Lucifer had the ability to still be able to send forth his music into heaven as if he were there. The only thing he couldn't do was to offer the music to God's throne while he was on the earth. He had to go there himself and stand in the presence of God in order to play before Him. Everyone seemed to miss him while he was on earth, yet each time, before his return to heaven, there was a very high level of anticipation concerning his arrival. This seemed to go on forever, and although there was an order to it, each time it happened was more spectacular than ever.

In Isaiah 14:13 the Lord spoke to His prophet concerning Lucifer. Also in Ezekiel 28:13 the prophet said that Lucifer was in Eden. Lucifer loved giving praise, worship, and glory to God. It was as if this was all he existed for. He would spend countless days in the sanctuary offering up the worship and praise of the earth and yet be just as excited bringing the angels the laws of God.

Chapter 5

Though it was barely recognizable, I soon noticed, to my shock and disbelief, that a change was taking place as the angels worshipped God and Lucifer played music. Over time, I began to see that Lucifer was very slowly changing their worship of God to worship of himself. In the past, he would just play the worship music, and everyone would come near the sanctuary as he sent the praise up to God. But now he was leading them away from the sanctuary to a place where he would be in the center, and it seemed like all the praises were being directed toward him. Because they knew his position in heaven, they never really questioned him about this change. They just accepted everything he said and did. At first he started by telling them that God wanted them to send their worship and praise toward him and that he would go into the sanctuary and offer it up to God. But when he left them and went into the sanctuary, instead of offering the worship and praise up to God, he would just stand there, caught up in what he had done. He started listening more and more to himself and admiring his own beauty. He slowly started changing laws concerning the earth, and soon he was telling the angels to give him glory. He told them that God wanted them to give him praise and that they should listen to him exclusively. Now he was talking about himself, what he wanted to do, and where he would go; everything was focused on him. In the past, when God would summon him, he would immediately appear before the throne, and when he would arrive, he would fully bow down and worship God in that position. But now, even though he came quickly, it was not as quickly as before. Next he started telling untruths concerning God. He was now saying that God didn't really care about them, because if He did, they would be allowed to walk before Him on the throne. He told them that God was about to create some new angels who would have more authority and be in a better position than theirs. He said that God was getting weaker. At first, none of the angels believed him or even listened to him, but as time went on and there was no response or reaction from God, it became very puzzling to them. One thing I noticed almost immediately from the time Lucifer started this trend of disobedience was that right above God would be a picture of everything Lucifer thought or did. At first I was puzzled as to why God didn't react and shut down this rebellion instantly. Then I remembered that He was omnipotent, omnipresent, and omniscient—why should he be concerned with this little act of treason? He's God. He knows everything from the beginning to the end.

I couldn't help but think about His mercy. When Adam and Eve sinned, He had mercy. When Cain slew Abel, He had mercy. Even when wicked Ahab repented in sackcloth and ashes, He showed mercy. Moses killed a man, and He had mercy. When Israel sorely sinned against God, He often showed mercy. In the love He showed for me when He allowed His only begotten Son to be crucified in my stead was mercy. What else would one expect of God? Who can know the mind of God? Who can be His counselor? You or I would have reacted right away, but He chose not to. Still, this whole thing baffled me. When Adam and Eve sinned, He could have destroyed them and started over, effectively preventing the mess we're in today, but He chose not to. He had a plan—a plan of redemption. After that, I realized God's greatness and power. But each day, Lucifer seemed to be getting bolder and bolder, trying to cause division among the angels. Then he started doing the unthinkable. When God would summon him to the throne, each time he purposely took more time to arrive. Now, when he arrived and bowed down, you could see something changing on his face. On his face was utter contempt for God. Each time he was called to the throne, he wouldn't bow as low as before. His sheer disrespect for God Almighty made me so angry. I wanted to see him destroyed immediately. Soon he stopped bowing down altogether and just started bending his head toward God. The next thing he did made me think God would surely make a move to destroy him: now, when God would summon him to the throne, he would send another angel. This was detestable, for he knew that the angel wasn't allowed to walk before the throne. When the angel would come back, telling Lucifer that he wasn't allowed to be in God's presence, Lucifer would say, "I don't know what happened, for He asked for you."

By now the situation on earth and in heaven seemed to be getting tense. Angels were now openly wondering why God hadn't stepped in and stopped Lucifer. They had never before seen this part of God, and it was difficult to bear. Lucifer soon stopped going into the sanctuary altogether. He now told the angels to worship and praise him only. He soon started bringing forth his own laws, which were contrary to God's. Angels on earth began offering him the same type of worship and praise that they offered God. I don't know whether the angels noticed, but slowly, Lucifer's appearance started to change. His music was also sounding different—repulsive, eerie, and frightening. His once majestic looks were slowly changing into something not so majestic and not so beautiful.

Soon, all of the earth was in an uproar over Lucifer. He started telling them that he was God and that he would sit on the throne in the north, high above the stars and clouds.

He began making all types of promises to his angels, telling them that there would be no difference between him and them and that they would be allowed to walk before the throne. They believed him, thinking he must have been right, because if God was more powerful, surely by now He would have responded. But strange as it may seem, the Father did absolutely nothing. Even when Lucifer stopped bowing down before His throne and started looking directly into His face with the most contemptible look imaginable, God showed no reaction. I wanted to cry at what I was experiencing, and I felt helpless to do anything other than to watch. The rush now taking place on earth and in heaven was almost unbearable. This was out-and-out mutiny on Lucifer's behalf. How dare he? How could he? Why would he? How long was this spectacle going to last?

He was planning for an all-out war against heaven, to take what he declared was rightfully his. I realized it was no longer a question of whether he would do it. No. Now the question was when. He had his angels in a frenzied hysteria, anticipating the next move in heaven.

Just when you thought everything would explode, he did the unimaginable: he erected his own throne and took a seat on it. At seeing this act of high treason, his angels went mad with exuberance and joy, worshipping and giving him praise in a way that looked distorted. They were rocking back and forth violently, yelling, "Lucifer is God! Lucifer is God! He is God!" They did this continuously, both day and night, and Lucifer just sat there enjoying it with this strange, sick grin on his face. The more they worshipped and praised him, the more he enjoyed it.

But for me, watching this became more and more sickening.

All of heaven was quiet, for the angels had never seen this before, and they couldn't comprehend why God was allowing this to take place. Just when you thought everything would explode, Lucifer stood up on the throne, looked up into heaven, and said the words that would change his course forever: "I will ascend into heaven. I will exalt my throne above the stars of God. I will sit also upon the mount of the congregation in the sides of the north. I will ascend above heights of clouds. I will be like The Most High" (Isaiah 14:13–14).

God, I thought, *do something. Don't You see what he's planning to do? Don't You know what he wants? He doesn't just want Your position—he wants You destroyed! Please react! Do something!* But as I looked at the throne, I saw that God hadn't changed His position at all. He was acting as if nothing was about to happen. *God, please, please, at least call your heavenly angels. Call Michael and his angels so that they can at least be on guard.* Lucifer and his angels headed straight toward heaven and God, planning to overthrow it. Then as I looked into heaven, I saw something marvelous—something that made me want to shout, cry, and yell. I just can't explain my emotions at that time. I saw that all the angels in heaven were ready! They were always ready. Their appearance changed into something superb! They looked bigger and stronger and more arrayed in color than before. It looked as if they were wearing some kind of heavenly armor. There was excitement in the air! I was too stunned to react; I could only watch.

I saw God standing up on His throne. I had never seen Him like this before. He had the look of one million conquerors all rolled up into one—not just a conqueror, but a conqueror of conquerors.

All of heaven was on display, and it was simply magnificent. The music was so wonderful, beautiful, and very powerful—the type of music you would hear after someone has conquered the universe.

I saw Michael and his angels at the entrance of heaven. Michael's appearance was so spectacular, arrayed like never before, and he had this look of total confidence and victory as he awaited Lucifer.

By this time, Lucifer and his angels were just about to enter into heaven. All of a sudden, I could see a change on Lucifer's face—a change from a look of victory, pride, and arrogance to one of utter confusion and fright. I realized that somehow Lucifer was being pulled toward God with an unbelievable force and speed. I saw Lucifer trying to resist with every ounce of his strength but to no avail. He soon realized it was useless. I also recognized that for every angel Lucifer had, God had about a million. His angels had no possible chance.

Lucifer was still trying to stop himself from being pulled toward the throne and God, but he simply couldn't. The closer he got to God, the more fear and fright you could see on his face.

The next thing that happened really blew me away. It's nothing I could have fathomed in a million years. Just as Lucifer reached God on His throne, something happened within the Father. At first, I was bewildered at what I was seeing, but as I focused more and more, I saw this bright, radiant light come forth from God. As He came forth, I could not believe what I was seeing. *No! It can't be! How could this be?* I wanted to let out a yell, but I couldn't. *No, it couldn't be.* There was something gold engraved in His chest. *Yes, it is! Yes, it is!* I thought. The gold engraving simply said, "Jesus, Son of God." *Yes! Hallelujah!* But God began to say something, quoting Ezekiel 28:12–18:

> Thou sealest up the sum, full of wisdom and per-
> fect in beauty. Thou has been in Eden, the garden

of God; every precious stone was thy covering. The sardius, topaz and the diamond, the beryl, the onyx and the jasper, the sapphire, the emerald and the carbuncle and gold: the workmanship of thy tabrets and of thy pipes was prepared in thee in the day that thou wast created. Thou art the anointed cherub that covereth; and I have set thee so: thou wast upon the holy mountain of God; thou has walked up and down in the midst of the stones of fire. Thou wast perfect in thy ways from the day that thou wast created, till iniquity was found in thee. By the multitude if thy merchandise, they have filled the midst of thee with violence and thou has sinned: therefore I will cast thee as profane out of the mountain of God and I will destroy thee o covering cherub from the midst of the stones of fire. Thine heart was lifted up because of thy beauty, thou hast corrupted thy wisdom by reason of thy brightness: I will cast thee to the ground, I will lay thee before kings, that they may behold thee. Thou has defiled the sanctuaries by the multitude of thy iniquities, by the iniquity of thy traffick; therefore will I bring forth a fire from the midst of thee, it shall devour thee, and I will bring thee to ashes upon the earth in the sight of all them that behold thee.

By then Lucifer was dumbfounded and totally frightened. Jesus grabbed Satan as you would a stick and simply threw him out of heaven. At the same time, all of the angels who had rebelled with him were also thrown out of heaven and back toward the earth. I noticed that as they were falling backward, they started taking on other shapes and forms. Their appearances changed, and they began losing all their beauty and splendor. They started looking horrific and terrible. Their faces became unimaginably deformed. Their once beautiful, strong, magnificent features were now repulsive. Lucifer looked the worst, and his frightening features were beyond description. He was thrown past the earth into the lower parts of hell itself, where the level of darkness was like nothing anyone has ever viewed—unless you never receive Christ into your life, in which case you'll get a firsthand look.

Then, looking back into heaven, I saw a scene of total and absolute victory. The angels were rejoicing, worshipping, and praising God for the victory. There was now praise like never before toward God the Father, God the Son, and God the Holy Spirit. Then, surprisingly, all the angels went back into God the Father, and He stood at the throne alone. In an instant, God's appearance changed as He looked down toward the earth and all its inhabitants. I had never seen God look like this. The look of fury and anger in His eyes would make you tremble for fear. This look was deadening and cold. I would have expected this look from Him when Lucifer first started changing in his ways and actions toward God. It was as if everything stood motionless. Seeing His appearance like this was frightening. Just the look in His eyes was enough to scare anyone to death.

As He looked toward the earth, I noticed that the sun had stopped shining and the stars had started disappearing. Everything began to turn pitch-black. You could see the fallen angels running, frightened, scattering all over the earth. They were now going into the lower parts of the earth where Satan was, and in one instant, this once beautiful earth turned into ice. Everything instantly froze. I somehow realized that I was seeing what happened between Genesis 1 and Genesis 2. Let's take a moment and explore my findings to see what happened to Lucifer, the garden of Eden, and the earth.

Genesis 1:1 says, "In the beginning God created the heaven and the earth." Verse two says "and the earth was without form and void and darkness was upon the face of the deep and the Spirit of God moved upon the face of the waters." In Hebrew, the word for *beginning* is *bara*, which means "brought out of nothing." In Hebrew, the same word means "the dateless past." In other words, this verse says that in the dateless past, Elohim created the heavens and the earth. This verse is ageless because it has no beginning. Who knows when the beginning was?

Here we are also seeing the trinity, because the name *Elohim* is the plural word for *God*. Also, any Hebrew noun that ends in *im* is plural, which means the term "the heavens" signifies more than one heaven. The first heaven, found in Genesis 1:8, is the atmosphere. The second heaven, in Ephesians 6, is where the principalities and powers of the air live. The third heaven is where Paul went when he saw God.

Something has now happened, because verse two says, "And the earth was without form and void and darkness was upon the face of the deep and the Spirit of God moved upon the face of the water." Something is missing or not right. The Hebrew word for *was* is *haya*, which means *become*. Something begins to happen between verse one and verse two. Read Deuteronomy 32:4. There are four Scriptures that claim that anything God creates is perfect. Everything that God does is perfection. Isaiah 45:18 lets us know that God did not create the earth in vain. It was created to be inhabited, and it was a work of perfection. Here God uses three words: *created*, *formed*, and *made*. He "created" the heavens and "formed" and "made" the earth. Ecclesiastes 3:11 says again that everything God makes is beautiful and perfect, and Psalm 18:30 tells us the same thing. In Genesis 1:2, we see that something is not right, because now the earth is formless, empty, dark, and flooded: "The spirit of God moved upon the face of the waters." Verse three says, "And God said let there be light." The word *let* is introduced. *Let* is never a word of creation. It is a word of permission. Verse four says, "And God saw the light, that it was good and God divided the light from the darkness." Where did this light come from? There was no sun, no moon, and no stars. In verse six, God says, "Let there be a firmament in the midst of the waters and let it divide the waters from the waters." There had to be a flood, for here God is dividing waters from waters, which is restoring, not creating. He was restoring the atmosphere of the earth. Verse seven introduces the word *made*. This word is *asa* in Hebrew, which simply means to make or mold or form. This is not building. In verse nine it is used again—permission, not creation. God says, "Let the dry land appear," which must mean that the dry land was flooded with water. Permission! The word *let*, in verse fourteen, "lights in the firmament of heaven to divide the day from the night." God now restores the sun, moon, and stars. Therefore, Genesis 1, from verse three on, is the work of restoration, not creation. In Genesis 2, the earth is formless, dark, and empty.

If we look at Genesis 2:1–2, a few things take place: Lucifer's fall, war between God and Lucifer, the destruction of earth and its inhabitants (demons), and the fall of countless angels who are now bound up in the underworld, traitors found among the angels of God. Earth was destroyed because of Lucifer's rebellion.

In Job 9:1–7, God is so angry that He removes the mountains and overturns them, but He also shook earth out of place. The pillars that held the earth trembled, and He commanded the sun not to shine and shielded the stars. Verse eight is a verse of restoration. The same thing that happened in verse eight also happened in Genesis 1. Look at Jeremiah 4:23. The prophet had a vision where God allowed him to see what the earth looked like. Genesis 2:2 shows us the same things found in Genesis 1:2.

Genesis 2:2 is also the same as Job 9. Job saw something strange. He saw no man, but he saw birds. In verse twenty-six, he again saw no man. He saw an earth that was destroyed and also a fruitful place that was destroyed. Genesis 1 is the reverse of Jeremiah 4:23–26. God allowed this prophet to see the earth's destruction, not its restoration. Verse twenty-six mentions cities. He was watching the earth go from a fruitful place to a wilderness. Verse twenty-seven lets us know that although God made the earth desolate, He will once again rebuild or restore it. We see, then, that the earth was once habited and now *uninhabited*. Once fruitful, now unfruitful. Beautiful, now empty. Though earlier God said "Good," now He was upset and angry. Who was He angry with? Not creation. We now understand that when God came back in Genesis 1:2, He began to restore the earth.

In Isaiah 24 we see the exact same things we see in Genesis 1:2. Here the Lord turned the world upside down, and then inhabitants were scattered abroad. Who were these inhabitants? These are the same demons we fight today. Job 9 says the earth was flooded. In Genesis 1:9, God restored the earth to its original form. He took the waters that had flooded the earth, restores the atmosphere, and gathers the waters into one place, and the dry land appears. In verse two, the Holy Spirit comes moving upon the face of the waters. Remember, there was no sun shining, so there was no warmth. It was all frozen. Its destruction had been sudden. Science tells us that dinosaurs were destroyed instantly. In Siberia, a prehistoric elephant was still eating lunch when it was instantly frozen in the ice. In Job 38:7, we see that the angels were there. They were rejoicing, which means this happened after Lucifer's fall. The angels were created before this. When God restored the earth and laid its foundations again, the angels were there, watching. They had already been created. See 25–30. This is about the time the earth had no inhabitants on it. Here, God was talking about when the earth was green and fruitful. But in verse thirty we see destruction. He created the earth and then destroyed it, and now it was frozen. His presence warmed up the earth, and it melted the ice, beginning the process of restoration.

Psalm 104:5–6 talks about the flood—the pre-Adamic flood or the flood before Adam was created, not the flood of Noah. Verse five shows us how God in His anger covered the earth with a flood. Verse seven says God rebuked the waters, and in verse eight, the flood was removed in a moment. This was not the flood of Noah, because the flood of Noah was not rebuked, only the pre-Adamic one.

Now let's examine Lucifer. Isaiah 4:1–12 says he was in heaven. He weakened the nations—which means the nations had to exist. He had an evil desire to enter into his heart. He looked up and saw God on His throne. Where was Lucifer? On earth. If he said he would exalt his throne above the clouds, he had to have been below them. When he said, "I will exalt my throne," this means he had a kingdom. Verse fourteen confirms once again that he was below the clouds. When he said, "I will be like the Most High God" in verse fifteen, God responded by saying that Lucifer would be brought down to hell, to the sides of the pit. This confirms that the Devil and his demons were in hell before Adam and Eve were created. We understand that the beings in verse sixteen were the demons in the pit—not human beings, but the demons who were destroyed in the rebellion.

Ezekiel 25:15 talks about Eden, the garden of God. There are two Edens, pre-Adamic and Adamic. The pre-Adamic Eden belonged to Lucifer, the Adamic to Adam.

Lucifer was the head of worship. Music came from within him.

He had two positions, one of archangel and one of cherub. Only Christ has more than one office in heaven. Lucifer was honored above all other angels. He was the anointed cherub who covered. The Word says he was anointed. He walked up and down in the midst of the stones of fire (Exodus 24:10–17). He was privileged to walk up and down before the throne of God. He was perfection itself, the worshipper of the godhead. He was the ruler of the earth with one-third of the angelic host. Their job was to give the worship of the earth to God and the laws of God to the earth. In verse seventeen, we see that there were kings, inhabitants, and cities on earth before Adam. God told Adam to replenish the earth, and He told Noah the same thing. This has to mean that it was once full; since it was empty, it needed to be refilled.

In verse eighteen, we see Lucifer was a priest, since he defiled his sanctuaries. Thus, he had more than one office. According to Isaiah, Lucifer was a king, for he had a throne, and a priest, for he had a sanctuary. He was also a prophet, giving God's Word to the nations. He corrupted God's Word and kept the angels' worship to himself. He was able to influence the whole world against God. He finally rebelled and invaded heaven. He fell. Hopefully this demonstrates not only what took place in Genesis 1 and 2 but also what Satan did after he fell to the earth and into hell.

Let's get back to my revelation. What I saw in one moment of time simply amazed me to the point where it seemed like I was in a trance. The entire earth, once this beautiful, magnificent place, was now completely frozen and suspended in time. Instantly, it was over. There was nothing left that was not pure ice—ice as it has never been seen before. Every single living creature was frozen in time. There was absolutely nothing left that wasn't frozen.

I remember that just before Lucifer's fall and total rebellion, I noticed a change in the behavior of prehistoric animals. Earlier

I mentioned all of these animals, both large and small, that somehow all cohabitated in total peace and harmony. It was truly a marvelous sight to behold, wonderful and amazing, for I knew that this was only possible by the power of God. But then they slowly became very angry and vicious toward each other. This once docile animal community was now turned into a ferocious, frenzied, meat-starved jungle. I believe that just as I started to see a change in Lucifer's behavior and countenance, this whole spirit of rebellion changed—not only among the angels but also among the animal population. Lucifer's rebellion affected everything that he was in contact with. It's hard to believe, but it's true. In God's anger and fury, everything Lucifer controlled paid a high price for *his* high treason.

After God turned His once perfect handiwork into what now looked like a frozen wilderness, He simply sat back down on His throne. Every angel in heaven who saw what was going on now began to worship and praise Him and give Him all the glory. I just want to take a minute to say that in no way, shape, or form am I trying to bring on confusion concerning the Word. Just search the Scriptures for yourself, and the Holy Spirit will show you the truth. I never asked for nor sought this revelation. The Holy Spirit gave it to me. What happened next, I can't explain; I can only tell you.

The next sight I saw was Jesus on the cross. All of heaven was motionless. I could see legions of angels just waiting near the cross. Then, as I looked upon the cross, I couldn't bear what I was seeing, for it was extremely sad. The last time I had seen Jesus, when He came forth from His Father, it was a picture of absolute splendor, majesty, and glory. But now to look at Him was almost impossible, for He looked nothing like He had earlier. Now I could see that He had been beaten and tortured beyond recognition. At one point, I had to turn my head away because of the brutal way He was beaten. Why did they do this to Him, and what did He do to deserve this type of inhumane treatment? His entire back was shredded to pieces, and His front had fared no better. This was very sad and hard to stomach. It made me sick just to look upon Him. There was blood everywhere. What could be in the hearts of men to devise this type of punishment? What I saw was so terrible, so horrific, that for as long as I'm on the earth, I will never, ever forget the image of Him on the cross.

I could feel myself getting angrier and angrier at what I was looking at. Then, as I looked near the cross, I could see the faces of the angels. I thought I had been so affected by this sight, but the looks on their faces made me weep. They had no choice but to watch their Christ be brutally and sadistically beaten. Can you just imagine how they felt watching Him suffer? Never before in time had they had to experience something of this magnitude, and never again will they. They were waiting for Him to just give them the word to rescue Him, to free Him, to relieve Him of this brutal torture—but you know what? It never came. They watched in sheer disbelief and pain as He uttered not a word. My God, why didn't He just give them the signal and let it be over? Why did He just stay there and suffer? I wanted to go to the cross myself and just take Him down and comfort Him. He looked so pitiful hanging there. It was totally unbearable, yet for some reason, I couldn't take my eyes from Him. What one prophet said was so true: "He was like a sheep before her shearers, like a lamb before the slaughter." He uttered not a word. The same prophet said, "He was wounded for our transgressions, He was bruised for our iniquities. The chastisement of our peace was upon Him and with His stripes, we are healed." He was right when he said, "There was no comeliness about Him that we should desire Him. He looked at His angels and then He just looked away."

Then I realized that a noise was coming from the crowds. They were taunting Him, teasing Him, mocking Him, and laughing at Him. The soldiers were gambling for His robe. Those people's behavior made me so sick, angry, and frustrated. Wasn't it enough that He'd been betrayed? Wasn't it enough that He'd been falsely accused? Wasn't it enough that He had been condemned? Wasn't it enough that He had been tortured? Wasn't it enough that He had nails in His hands and feet? Wasn't it enough that He wasn't even recognizable? Wasn't it enough that He had been found innocent by Pilate? But because of that spirit of hatred for Him, they demanded He be crucified. What more did they want or expect? They knew that He would soon be dead. And then, in spite of suffering and being tortured—I don't know how He did it or whether He even had the strength to utter words—He kept silent to His angels. But I heard Him say something that was so typical of Him. He responded to the thief's comments on the cross, in spite of His own pain, suffering, and despair. In that moment, He seemingly forgot about Himself. I don't believe anyone else could do this. You or I probably would have looked at this person as if He had lost His mind or something. We would have replied to Him with something like, "Are you stupid and blind? Don't you see my condition? Can't you see all the blood I've lost? Man, I'm barely conscious. Leave me alone, that I may die!" No, not our Lord and Savior. No, not Jesus Christ. He looked over at the man with those compassionate, loving, and caring eyes and said to him, "Today, thou shalt be with Me in paradise." The Bible gives no history on this man. Did he know before that moment who Jesus was? Had he heard any of His sermons? Had he seen any of His miracles? With Jesus, it didn't matter. All that mattered was that at that moment, he recognized who He was and simply said, "Have mercy on me," and those four words allowed him to change his destiny.

Again, I was able to look down into hell, and to my shock and dismay, there was Satan, sitting on his throne. He was intensely watching what was going on, and he had a look of absolute disdain and contempt for the Lord. His chief demons were surrounding his throne. Most of the demons in hell were worshipping and praising Satan and giving him all the glory for what was going on. Then, all of a sudden, Satan let out this loud, sadistic snarl. It sounded like a beast. He started laughing and telling his demons, "Didn't I tell you so? Didn't I tell you so? I told you I would do it! I told you I would get even with Him for what He did to me. I told you I would have revenge for what He did to me. I told you I would make Him sorry for challenging me." I could see that he was still so very bitter and angry: in all that he said, he didn't even acknowledge Him as God.

Next I witnessed hysteria that would make you sick. Everyone in hell began to let out unbearable yowls and screams sickening to the ear. All were waiting for the entrance of Jesus. They believed that once there, He would be held captive with those who died believing in God. They were having a precelebration of the Lord's entry into these parts.

Just as I couldn't bear it any longer, my attention was turned back to the cross as I heard Jesus say, "Father, why hast thou forsaken me?" The way He said it made all who heard it feel a sense of utter hopelessness for Jesus. I immediately looked up to the throne, and to my surprise and bewilderment, I saw that the throne was empty. I was startled and dumbfounded. Where was God? Where could He be? Why did He leave? What was going on? At Jesus' most desperate hour of need, the throne was empty. I then noticed that everything in heaven had come to a complete standstill—no worship, no music, no praise, no one giving God the glory. At that moment, absolutely nothing was going on in heaven. At that point, Jesus had no support system—nothing, nobody, no one.

Thomas Jones

I saw something coming toward Jesus. What was it? I didn't understand what was going on. What could this be? Whatever it was, it was dark and evil. The closer it moved to Jesus, the more on edge I felt. Now it began to wrap itself around the body of Jesus in an unnatural way. Its appearance was ugly and repulsive. Somehow I knew that it was the garment that carried the sins of the world. Any believer who witnessed this would not have been able to hold back his or her emotions. I was reminded of my own sins, disobedience, rebellious ways, and sicknesses. I couldn't help but praise Him and give Him the glory. I remembered the Scripture in Isaiah that says, "He was wounded for my transgressions; He was bruised for my iniquities. The chastisement of our peace was upon Him and with His stripes we are healed." I don't believe we as Christians fully comprehend what Christ actually did for us. When Adam and Eve sinned, they altered the destiny of humanity. Because of their sin, God now required payment that would satisfy what sin had accomplished. He could have easily destroyed them and started over, but He didn't. To me, this would have been the easy way out—to simply get rid of these two who rebelled and disobeyed God. Some of you might argue they didn't rebel, but they did. Anytime God tells you something that you shouldn't do and also tells you what the consequences of your disobedience will be, and, in spite of all this information, you still do it, this is clearly an act not only of rebellion, but also of treason. When Saul disobeyed God, Samuel told him that rebellion was like the sin of witchcraft. He also told him that obedience was better than sacrifice.

Despite what Adam and Eve did, God did not destroy them. In this decision, we see those same characteristics and ways He made known to Moses when he asked God to "show me thy glory" in Exodus 38:18. I now more fully understand why He asked the Father three times to "let this cup pass from Me." He knew that

34

there would come a moment on the cross when something He had never experienced would have to take place—something that, for the first time ever, would force the Father to pull away. That's why He agonized and cried drops of blood. Yet He still said "Nevertheless, not My will, but Thine be done," for He knew that at the moment His Father just wouldn't just draw back, but totally separate Himself from His beloved Son. It wasn't even the pain of the crucifixion or the merciless beatings He would have to endure en route to the cross. He wasn't even concerned about death, for He Himself said, "No man taketh My life from Me. I lay it down Myself. I have the power to lay it down and the power to take it back up again" (John 10:18). Remember, He always said that His will was to do the will of His Father (John 4:34, 5:30, 6:38). He forever lives to please His Father. Everything He ever did, He always pointed back to the Father. He gave His Father all the glory all the time. It's a wonderful thing when you see children who simply want to please their parents in all that they do, both in all their actions and in their ways, no matter what. But we know it's impossible to live up to these standards, because the Word says, "There is no perfect, no, not one." We also know that failing and making mistakes are vital pieces of the learning process. But none of that applies to Jesus. He was tempted on all points but was without sin. He was the sinless sacrifice. With all the love God had for His Son, He seems to have an even greater love for us—undeserving, rebellious, sinful man. That's why His love for us is expressed in John 3:16. God loved us so much that He allowed His only begotten Son, who was perfect, sinless, and blameless, to become our sacrificial lamb so that He could take on Himself the sins of the world, which would satisfy what God required as payment for man's fall.

We can see how difficult it must have been for God to know that there would come a time when He would have to abandon

His only beloved Son and that, in that moment, His Son would feel the pain of a son being deserted by his father. Jesus had never before spent one moment without the fellowship that He knew to be more precious than life itself, but He was willing to do whatever the Father asked of Him, no matter the suffering and pain He had to endure.

The next voice I heard was that of Jesus saying, "It is finished" (John 19:30). All of heaven seemed to be in a state of shock at what was taking place; the angels' faces looked puzzled and uneasy. It was as if you could hear them saying, "Where is He? Where is the Son of God?" And at that moment I realized that God was on the throne, and with His presence, there came a spirit of worship and praise that brought calm to all of heaven.

Just then, my attention was taken back down into hell. All the demons were in a state of frenzy and hysteria. They were acting like wild beasts. I could see some sort of disgusting foam coming from their mouths. It was repulsive. They were all yelling, "It's over! It's over!" I could see they were anticipating Jesus' arrival. Satan had this disturbed, distorted look on his face, as though he had conquered all the universe. He looked like he knew he had finally affected God and that He wouldn't be able to recover. Ever since the fall, he had been waiting for the chance to hurt God.

Now he spoke aloud to his demons. "What a victory! What a triumph!" At this, they started worshipping him like never before, and I could see he enjoyed it. He said, "Jesus Christ, the Son of God, is now trapped, never to be freed!"

Let's get back to the revelation, to the story of Lazarus and the rich ruler. When Lazarus died, the Bible says he woke up in the arms of Abraham, but the rich ruler lifted his eyes in hell. The Bible also lets us know that although they could see each other, there was still a separation of those who had died trusting God and those who hadn't. Somehow the ruler was able to look over to

Abraham and Lazarus, for he asked if Lazarus could dip the tip of his finger in water and cool his tongue, "for I am tormented in this flame." Abraham said, "There is a great gulf between us, so that they that would pass from hence to you cannot. Neither can they pass to us, that would come from thence" (Luke 16:24–26). So by this, we can conclude that the resting place for believers was made in such a way that although you could see over into hell, you were not affected by its torment and what the nonbelievers felt.

Satan was just happy to have Jesus trapped in this resting place, thinking that it didn't matter as long as He was the Son of God. That was important. Now I was starting to wonder where Jesus was and what had happened, but before my thoughts went any further, I began to see into hell. I told you earlier about its darkness, terrible odors, and frightening feeling. I now saw something that I hadn't noticed before—all types of demons, all of whom looked so frightening and horrible. Just the sight of them sent chills through me. There were also worms everywhere, seemingly as many worms as demons, and they were disgusting.

I could hear loud yelling and troublesome screaming. The demons were going crazy, waiting for Jesus, but I couldn't see clearly because of the level of darkness. It sounded like people were being tormented in an unimaginable way. I began to feel sorry for the voices I heard but couldn't see.

All the demons in hell had gathered around Satan's throne to wait together for Jesus' entry. I could now see better. I couldn't even count the demons for multitude. It seemed like the demons nearer to Satan's throne were even eerier and more horrible than the others. They also seemed more powerful and hideous, features-wise.

Suddenly I noticed a tiny light way in the back of hell. This light was moving forward very slowly. All the frenzy and hysteria began to subside, as everyone seemed to sense something unusual.

The closer the light came to the front, the more I felt that they knew something was terribly wrong. Demons began looking back and forth between themselves and Satan. Even he was motionless on his throne.

As the light came closer and closer, I saw the demons become even more hysterical. It wasn't like before when they were celebrating Satan's victory over Jesus as they awaited His entry. No, this was quite different. They were literally acting crazy, appearing to experience torment and pain. The demons started moving very violently and uncontrollably. All at once, a sudden fear came upon them. Now, as their bodies continued to shake, the speed of their movements picked up, becoming fast and violent. I looked over to Satan, who was still sitting on his throne, but with a puzzled look on his face, unsure what was going on. Even when he commanded them to stop, for some reason they could not.

As the light kept getting closer, they did something I did not understand at first, but the more I looked, the more I saw and understood what was taking place. The demons started bowing toward the ground, and once they had bowed down, they could not get up. I saw Satan grab both sides of his throne in anger as he watched what was taking place. I then began to understand what they had been uttering. They were saying, "Jesus is Lord! Jesus is Lord!" over and over and over again.

At the sound of that name, Satan furiously jumped up from his throne. The anger, frustration, and disgust could be seen in his eyes. But now the light was approaching the throne, and Satan's features began changing. Looking at him, I realized that at no point in my life had I ever witnessed anything so frightful. Satan's body moved back and forth, but he fought it. The closer the light came, the more he fought it, and he suddenly froze. I could now see what this light was. Then it started all over again, and again demons bowed. The contortions of Satan's face were visible as he tried with all of his might to keep this power from overtaking him. I knew what was happening. Satan, Lucifer, the Devil, the accuser of the brethren, the deceiver, the Father of Lies, the former archangel and cherub, the former holder of light, he who used to walk before God—he was bending toward the floor! The more he resisted, the closer he came to the ground. Somehow, just before his head went fully down, I saw his thoughts. They kept returning to his time in heaven and in the presence of the Father. He thought about every time he came into God's presence and automatically bowed down in reverence, beginning to worship, praise, and adore God.

At that time, the light appeared, and I saw that the light was Jesus Christ! I became so excited at His appearance that I could have burst open. He was now wearing a crown that said "King of kings." On His chest were the words "Lord of lords." As Satan bowed down to the ground, I could not make out what he uttered. I initially thought that maybe he was cursing God in his anger and fury, even though he was bowing. However, I soon realized that he was also saying, "Jesus is Lord! Jesus Christ is Lord!" I remembered the Scripture that says, "Every knee shall bow, and every tongue shall confess that Jesus Christ is Lord to the glory of God the Father."

I heard the Lord say to Lucifer, "You know why I'm here." By this time, Satan was bowing down at the feet of Jesus in front of his own throne. Though I hadn't seen it before, I noticed something hanging right above Satan's throne, in the midst of those horrific worms. There were the keys of death and the grave. I became so elated as the Lord reached over and snatched the keys from above Satan's throne. I saw Satan's anger and frustration at not being able to do anything except continue to confess that Jesus Christ is Lord.

Now able to see another section of the underworld, I was fully astonished to witness people going into a state of mass hysteria—but in a good way. This was excitement like nothing I had ever seen. At first I didn't understand what was going on, but as my vision became clearer, I knew. Everyone there knew! First I saw Adam, and he was asking Eve if she'd heard that voice. He kept asking her over and over again. She said yes, and they began to weep. I saw as it was in the garden of Eden when they'd communed with God in the cool of the day (Genesis 3:8), recognizing His voice. I saw Abraham and Sarah, and they too were asking each other the same question: "Did you hear that voice? Did you hear that voice?" Then I remembered when God spoke to them both in Genesis 18:13–15. There was Isaac (Genesis 26:24), Jacob (Genesis 35:10), Moses (Exodus 3:4), and everyone else the Lord had spoken to at one time. They were all excited and asking each other that same question: "Did you hear that voice?" And the response was always "Yes!" Everyone was shouting, praising, and worshipping Jesus. I had tears of joy in my spirit. Everyone was so excited at hearing His voice.

When He appeared and I looked at His face, He had this look of joy and satisfaction. For a moment, I thought He might weep. At his appearance all were immediately bowing down and saying, "Jesus is Lord! Jesus Christ is Lord!" I wish you could have seen this most heartfelt and beautiful sight. The Lord, just by being there, comforted them like a mother who had been away from her children for a while but was now back to take care of them forever.

He told them the story of redemption and of His Father's plan that would redeem man from the grip of Satan. When He finished telling them the redemption story, He asked them if they were ready, and without saying a word, I knew this was the moment they all had been waiting for. Instantly, they started going up toward heaven. As they went up, I could see things falling back down toward earth. It looked like presents, but I remembered the

Scripture that says, "He led captivity captive and He gave gifts unto man." I was filled with such exuberance that it felt like I could not take any more of the joy I felt.

But my excitement again turned to fear as I looked back at hell and the area around Satan's throne. He and all his demons were cursing and blaspheming God, His Son, and the Holy Spirit. They were in a frenzied state once again, looking twice as bad as before. My body was chilled at the sight of them, because they looked even more distorted than they previously had. Satan was looking up toward heaven, repeatedly cursing the godhead. He said in a hideously loud voice, "It's not over! You think You won. Just wait and see. I'm still the prince of this world. How dare You invade my kingdom! How dare You! I vow to kill and destroy everyone who believes in You. I'm still in control! You just wait and see." Then, there was sudden, terrifying silence. All of hell was motionless for a good sixty seconds. Satan let out a laugh that grew harder and harder, louder and louder, eventually becoming sickening to the ear.

My attention was then brought back to heaven, whose entrance Jesus was approaching. The great anticipation of His return was palpable, with all of heaven seeming ecstatic. There was unbelievable worshipping, praising, and giving glory to God, yet it was so sweet and satisfying. Everything and everyone was giving God the glory. Even the sun, moon, and stars appeared to be in sheer excitement. It was as if they were alive and knew what was going on. It looked like a trillion times a trillion angels were celebrating Jesus' return. The Lord looked like a mighty conqueror. He truly looked like the King of kings and the Lord of lords. Yet, in spite of all this, there was still this marvelous, magnificent look on His face that showed forth His humility in a way indescribable. There was no look of arrogance, conceit, or pride on His face—only the look of a son who simply wanted to please his father.

Looking toward the throne, I saw that the Father had a look that would bring tears to anyone's eyes. He had a look of satisfaction, happiness, joy, and pride as one has never seen before. He was standing up on His throne as His beloved Son came closer. God had a Son who had done everything right in life with no letdowns, and the plans and promises He'd made were kept and followed exactly as He'd been given them. Although there were difficult and sometimes impossible odds against Him, he was always successful. There may have been times when any parent would have accepted a child saying, "I'm sorry, but it's too much. I can't go on with it." But no. In spite of everything, Jesus was faithful and fulfilled His assignment to bring us back into full fellowship with the Father, in nothing but total victory, praise be to God.

I remembered what the apostle Paul said in 2 Timothy 4:6–7: "For I am now ready to be offered and the time of my departure is at hand. I have fought a good fight. I have finished my course, I have kept the faith." Just then, Jesus stepped forth and looked at His Father, and at once the Father came down from the throne and accompanied Jesus over to the mercy seat. While the Father looked on and all of heaven kept silent, Jesus put His own blood that He'd shed for the world inside the mercy seat, and at that very moment, heaven let out a loud and jubilant cheer. I believe that if the entire world had witnessed this momentous event, there wouldn't have been a dry eye anywhere on this planet—for Jesus, by shedding His blood, had successfully paid what God the Father required when Adam sinned.

God and His Son Jesus walked back toward the throne, and the Father motioned for Him to sit on His right side. When Jesus took His seat and turned again, I saw that He was now also wearing a banner that read "High Priest and Great Intercessor." I began to praise God for allowing us to have a High Priest and great intercessor who always pleads our cases.

Epilogue

You know, when I completed this revelation from the Holy Spirit, that very night I was attacked by demonic spirits as I slept. I now realize without a shadow of a doubt that what was given to me was supposed to reveal Satan for who he was, what he did, and the ultimate contempt and disdain he has for God, Jesus, and the Holy Spirit. What the Lord did was unveil unto us more information about him than ever before.

The night I finished this story, my wife asked me to read it to her. As I did, I found myself crying at times. I was simply amazed, because although He had given me this revelation to write, it seemed as if I was hearing it for the first time. I have no explanation of how this was possible, but that's exactly what I felt.

Earlier in the story, I mentioned something about the last great revival. I believe that we are actually living in the last days and that Christ is coming back soon. No, I don't know exactly when, but if I could put a number on it, I would say within the next thirty years. I've felt this way since just after my conversion nearly twenty-five years ago. I never believed I would taste physical death as we know it, but I believe that I will be caught up to meet Him in the air. I know many of you will say, "Oh, yeah. We've heard that before." We the church have to stop and examine the times that we're living in and realize what the only thing is that could potentially be holding back the rapture. Everything possible is in place for His return except one thing. That is very simple. We're just not ready. If He came right now, at this present moment, so many would be lost for all eternity, both believers and nonbelievers. There are ministers everywhere you turn. With television, church can be found 24/7. There are more faithful, prosperous, Word-driven, healing, praise-giving, worship-offering, tongue-speaking churches now than at any other time on our history. Yet, with all this, why aren't people coming to Christ by the millions? We've been our own worst enemy, and we've simply lost the effect and the power that the early church had.

I read this story about the Catholic Church. One of the higher officials was having a conversation with one of the cardinals, and he said, "No longer can we say, 'Silver and gold have I none,' seeing that we are possibly the richest denomination in the world." The cardinal replied, "Yes, you're right." But he said, "No longer can we say 'Rise up and walk," either." This hit the nail right on the head. The church is no longer operating the way it's supposed to. Whether you want to admit it or not, we've lost that connection. There may be no more than a few ministries operating with the kind of power and anointing that Jesus said we would have. I'm not pointing fingers or blaming anyone. I'm just telling you what you all already know deep down in your hearts.

There are countless ministries out there who are truly preaching and teaching the unadulterated word of God in an effective way, but still people are not flocking to the churches like they should be.

We need to ask ourselves one question: What is the number-one reason the multitudes came to see and hear Jesus? It wasn't so much the work or how He fed them. No, beloved. It was for one reason and one reason only. They heard about the miracles. You can argue, debate, fuss, fight, or get upset, but once you've calmed down, taken a deep breath, and really thought about it, if you study His early ministry, you will have to conclude that what

I just said is true. Therefore, I believe that the key thing that will usher in the explosion of nonbelievers into the church is one last great revival. I believe that what caused people to flock to Jesus and His apostles were the miracles, and I've had this belief down in my spirit for over twenty years. Even when I would preach, I would always find myself saying these things. But now more than ever before, I am certain that these things will come to pass. Not only do people need to hear the Word of God, but they also need to experience the power of the Holy Spirit manifested through miracles, signs, and wonders. No nonbeliever in his right mind would refute who Jesus is if he were exposed to this.

I know that some will say that this period is over and that all they need is the God's Word and Spirit. But you have to remember what it was like when Jesus was here. First of all, He was God in the flesh. Secondly, though He was the Word made flesh, everywhere He went, He healed and delivered people and set them free. His ministry started with a miracle: turning water into wine. He came to do the will of the Father. As a matter of fact, Jesus Christ was the will of God in action. The Bible says that He healed and set people free everywhere He went. He said, "The works that I do, a greater work than these shall you do, because I go to my Father." Again, I know some are going to say that He meant communications, media, etc. Yes, but that's just a part of it. If we let people hear that there are real miracles, signs, and wonders taking place, we would have people flocking by the millions to see it.

After Jesus performed these miracles, He would always teach and preach the Word. I said all of that to say this: I believe that this last great revival is for one purpose and one purpose only, and that is to usher in the kingdom, millions upon millions of nonbelievers and Christians who are not in their rightful places. And when that happens, I believe that the Lord will immediately usher in the rapture. It will be like an exodus of believers, all in a position to meet Him in the air. What else will cause people to believe in Jesus Christ the Word?

Again, there is more Word being preached now than at any time in history. It's going to take the pure, raw power of the Holy Spirit to release signs, wonders, and miracles and usher in the largest-ever number of believers into the kingdom at one time. And when all that is completed, I believe we will see the return of the Lord.

This once again demonstrates the total, absolute love God has for His people. His will is that no man should perish, but have everlasting life.

Yours truly,
Thomas Jones

Printed in the United States
By Bookmasters